The Critical Mind

Enhance Your Problem Solving, Questioning, Observing, and Evaluating Skills

Zoe McKey

Communication Coach and Social Development Trainer

zoemckey@gmail.com
www.zoemckey.com

understanding that the author is not engaged in rendering medical, legal or other professional advice or services. If professional assistance is required, the services of a competent professional person should be sought. The author shall not be liable for damages arising herefrom. The fact that an individual, organization of website is referred to in this work as a citation and/or potential source of further information does not mean that the author endorses the information the individual, organization to website may provide or recommendations they/it may make. Further, readers should be aware that Internet websites listed in this work might have changed or disappeared between when this work was written and when it is read.

For general information on the products and services or to obtain technical support, please contact the author.

CREATED BY

ZOE MCKEY

SELF-DISCOVERY

~Starter Kit~

Thank you for choosing my book! I would like to show my appreciation for the trust you gave me by giving a **FREE GIFT** for you!

Visit www.zoemckey.com for more information.

The kit shares *10 key practices to help you to:*

- *discover your true self,*
- *find your life areas that need improvement,*
- *find self-forgiveness,*
- *become better at socializing,*
- *lead a life of gratitude and purpose.*

The kit contains extra actionable worksheets with practice exercises for deeper learning.

Table Of Contents

Introduction

Did you know that clothing made out of cotton is the healthiest for your skin? No, seriously, I'm telling you. *Believe me*. My grandmother said it, so it's true.

My friend, a bodybuilder, always washes his chicken meat before he cooks it. You should wash your chicken too. I mean, he's a bodybuilder, he eats chicken each day—he probably knows best.

I know for a fact that even the most intelligent people use only 10% of their brain's capacity. All the rest is wasted potential... Well, I read it in an article on a website called Bored Panda. I also saw that movie, *Lucy*...

Shall I go on, or have you given me enough credit already?

What about watermelon seeds causing appendicitis? Or the five-second rule when you drop your food on the ground? Or that lightning never strikes the same place twice?

The examples mentioned above are urban legends at best. Why do we invent them and believe them then? Because humans are wired to look for explanations for everything. We hate the unknown and love security. Thousands of years ago we tried to explain the unknown by attaching superhuman attributives to natural phenomena. Today, we try to get to the bottom of our questions using science. But we crave the need for an explanation.

We are also lazy and impatient. Therefore, we wish to get our explanation as quickly and as easily as possible.

That's why I never questioned my grandmother about her village knowledge about cotton. I didn't take the trouble to—first and foremost—check her age and involvement in contemporary science. When she was young in 1930, there might not have been alternative materials to cotton that resisted the hard washing procedure my great-grandmother and her mother before her put the clothes through. They literally cooked each cloth, from panties to bed sheets, in gigantic pots. As detergent, they used homemade soap they also cooked out of tallow or lard (or both). No germ could survive such an atrocity, I give them that. But since then, the clothing industry has developed a lot. Today there are breathable synthetic materials which are more optimized for different skin types than cotton. They are hypoallergenic, better for handling sweat, and so on.

The same goes for my bodybuilder friend. Since I saw him wash chicken, I also started washing chicken. Why? I believed he knew better because he cooked chicken more often than I did. Only, later, I researched the topic and I found that washing before cooking does not benefit the meat itself because the hot oil will kill everything possibly harmful. The chicken-water splashing around the sink, on the other hand, will stay in a lukewarm environment, helping the bacteria to thrive. So washing the chicken actually does more harm than good.

That popular belief about the brain? Wrong. Scientists have proven that we actually use 100% of our brain each day—just not at the same time.[i]

Today, it is easier to research information than ever before. However, at the same time, it is also easier to acquire false information. If we put a little effort into our thinking instead of accepting the first thing we hear or read automatically, we can reduce the possibility of being wrong.

Cogito ergo sum. "I think, therefore I am," said René Descartes. This famous conclusion was the end of the search the French philosopher carried out for a statement that could not be doubted. He discovered that he could not doubt his existence, as he was the one doing the doubting in the first place.

Let's take this analogy even further: *Dubito, ergo cogito, ergo sum.* "I doubt, therefore I think, therefore I am." Descartes discovered early on that it is possible to take a skeptical viewpoint on anything. The main message of his argument is that you can doubt almost everything about the world, but you can't doubt that you're doubting. Because if you doubt that you're doubting, you're still doubting.

Before we enter into deep philosophical debates, let me tell you why Descartes' message is important for this book:

"I doubt, therefore I think. However, 'I think' doesn't automatically imply that *I know.*"

Thinking and knowing are two different states of mind. Just because we think something doesn't make it knowledge—much less the truth.

Please question my words. Question your own words. Question the news, the latest statement from your father… Question what you hear.

Critical thinking is a way of thinking where you don't simply accept all arguments and conclusions. When you get exposed to new information, you approach it with a curious, questioning attitude. Critical thinking means making decisions and forming opinions based on reason and logic. You don't accept claims as the truth by default, rather, you seek the evidence supporting them.

This book discusses the best critical-thinking strategies and cognitive pathways that will lead you to the least wrong answer possible. Why didn't I say "the right answer?" Find out in this book. Learn to use your logic to the fullest, and make better decisions in business and your personal life.

Chapter 1: What is Critical Thinking?

"The philosopher Richard Paul has described three kinds of people: vulgar believers, who use slogans and platitudes to bully those holding different points of view into agreeing with them; sophisticated believers, who are skilled at using intellectual arguments, but only to defend what they already believe; and critical believers, who reason their way to conclusions and are ready to listen to others."

— Carole Wade and Carol Tavris

Critical thinking is a cognitive process spiced with questions like "How do you know that?" or "How did you come to this conclusion?" or "What is the evidence that supports that claim?" or "Are there any alternative possibilities to this theory?"

It sounds very obvious. You may think "That's it? I already know these questions." Sure. We all do. But how often do we actually use them?

Critical thinkers prioritize reasoned judgments over gut responses—logic over emotions. They don't sign up for arguments simply because someone said it, but rather have a questioning attitude. They are like the thought police—they want evidence.

Critical thinking requires three key qualities according to experts: curiosity, skepticism, and humility. I would like to add another very important skill that makes all the difference between a critical thinker who is a schmuck, and a critical thinker who is a helpful, guiding individual. This quality is kindness.

People who feed their critical mind are curious. What additional facts or unspoken words lie behind a statement? They are not only curious about whether or not the statement is true but also the motivation of the speaker who said that statement with such certainty.

Take my grandmother as an example. I had to take into consideration the era she grew up in, her age at which any "modern monster" invention was looked at with suspicion. I knew she meant well promoting cotton. She had good intentions. I also knew she was wrong. Did I tell her she was wrong? Of course not. This is where kindness plays a big role. I probably wouldn't have been able to convince my grandmother with any scientific paper or Nike Air outfit. Cotton was what she knew all her life; she felt happy and safe wearing cotton. Who was I to take that away from her? I accepted that my grandmother wanted to believe what she wanted to believe—she didn't ask for my help, so I just did my own research and left the topic alone.

Not everybody has good intentions when they are spreading unverified information. Take some news channels, for example. In Hungary there is a big anti-migration agenda going on right now. The two leading governmental TV channels, Duna TV and M1, reported about migration-related crimes in 36.7% and 37% of their news broadcasts in 2019.[ii] That is a ridiculous percentage because Hungary gives refuge for only a minimal amount of migrants. The number of refuge seekers has gradually decreased from 2015, when it peaked. In 2018 only 671 migrants requested refuge in Hungary and 367 were granted refuge. Thus we can hardly speak of a migrant crisis and "Islamization," two leading keywords in Hungarian domestic policy.[iii] A high percentage of the population is sold to hate this common enemy just because, thanks to human availability bias, they hear about it often enough. I or any of my friends had never had any bad experience because of these mythical migrants. But there is always that person in our friend circle, whose aunt's best friend's husband's mother-in-law's neighbor got mugged by a migrant. I'm not even saying they didn't. Some people mug other people, and some of them are migrants. But the disproportionate fear, hysteria, and hatred directed to this part of the population is alarming. Behind spreading this information lays the deliberate wish to alter the sense of reality and safety in the population. Regardless of how you feel about migration and migrants—I can accept whether you are pro-migration or against—the events in Hungary are frustrating to the critical mind because there is no migrant crisis.

Lack of curiosity can make people accept information without questioning it, and in some extreme cases it can lead to tragic outcomes. If one is curious but close-minded, they'll only hear out the new ideas that are in alignment with their pre-existing beliefs. That's not critical thinking, just a simple craving for confirmation bias.

Skepticism is the second skill that makes a good critical thinker. Skepticism doesn't equal being the annoying, hen-pecking person who tries to pick at and question everything every time. Skeptics rather have a healthy, well-timed, well-placed questioning attitude about new or unknown information. They don't blindly believe everything they hear. Without a healthy dose of skepticism, you can't think critically.

I wish to highlight the importance of kindness when it comes to expressing our skepticism. There are ways to tell people we have our doubts about what they are saying. Getting into someone's face, saying, "I have more knowledge about this topic and it doesn't make sense what you're saying. I don't believe it," will create some resentment in the receiver. Even if they are wrong, they'll stick to their guns now that their beliefs and sense of self was attacked. When we express skepticism it is better to acknowledge what the other person is saying, even if we disagree. Try to understand why it makes sense for the other person to say that. If you wish to express your skepticism, start by validating what the other said first. "I see why you see X topic this way." or "I wish to understand where you're coming from when you say X. Can you please elaborate on…?" Ask more information about the part you're skeptical about. This way your conversation partner will give you additional information without even knowing your skepticism. If the answer you get by digging deeper is satisfactory, good job. If, after an exhaustive explanation you still feel skeptical, decide what you want to do: find the truth out or convince the other person about her wrong? If the former, do your own research. Clearly, the person you're talking to believes what they already stated. If the latter, be prepared to hit a strong wall. People cherish their beliefs and feel threatened when someone questions them. Later in this book I will talk about how to express skepticism in a safe, non-confrontational way.

The third skill of critical thinkers is humility. Just like the other two skills, humility is also essential to possessing greater judgment. One has to be able to admit that their opinions were wrong and embrace the evidence. Curious skeptics without the ability to accept when they are wrong are called bullies.[iv]

Although critical thinking sounds like a dry and rigid kind of thinking, lacking any sort of creativity, that's far from being true. It actually challenges creative thinking. Without it, one couldn't come up with possible solutions or explanations to problems. Creative thinking connects the dots between objective facts and critical thinking. According to Carole Wade and Carol Tavris, the authors of the book *Critical and Creative Thinking*, one can't really separate critical and creative thinking. Only when you question "something given (critical thinking pathway)" can you start thinking about "what it could be (creative thinking pathway)."

If you fear that critical thinking will rob you of your charming, creative persona, it's time to question that belief. Critical thinking only takes your creativity to a different realm—the realm of reality.[v]

Qualities of a Critical Thinker

I'm a huge fan of lists. Even when it comes to qualities I'd like to adopt or improve in myself. According to the APA, the characteristics and qualities of critical thinkers are:

- "inquisitiveness with regard to a wide range of issues;
- concern to become and remain well-informed;
- alertness to opportunities to use critical thinking;
- self-confidence in one's own abilities to reason;

- open-mindedness regarding divergent world views;
- flexibility in considering alternatives and opinions;
- understanding of the opinions of other people;
- fair-mindedness in appraising reasoning;
- honesty in facing one's own biases, prejudices, stereotypes, or egocentric tendencies;
- prudence in suspending, making, or altering judgments; and a
- willingness to reconsider and revise views where honest reflection suggests that change is warranted"[vi]

This chapter shed light on some of the benefits of critical thinking. As you could see, it isn't the enemy of creativity and doesn't make you the next Dr. House. It simply arms you with thinking skills that can help you make better, more reasoned decisions.

Chapter 2: Piaget's Theory on Thinking

If you have a soft spot for psychology, you may have heard of Jean Piaget. However, if you steer clear of any and all psychology, you probably have no idea how to even pronounce the name (it's *pee-ah-jay*). How can a person you know hardly anything about be so important that a whole chapter is dedicated to them? It turns out that Piaget actually had some stuff going for him. Not only was he incredibly bright, but he shaped the way we think about human cognition.

I know, I know, there are some big words there. Don't worry, I'm going to explain it all. Piaget's theory had four different stages, which he called "operational stages." These start from birth and go into the ripe old age of adulthood. He said that when we are born, we start in the first stage. Piaget established the four stages, and he used those four stages to determine differences in intelligence.

Piaget also believed that children were like little scientists. So when that chubby-faced one-year-old rolls a ball down a hill and observes the outcome, they make a note in their mind that if they push the ball down a hill, it will roll and keep going. They conduct these small "experiments" throughout their daily play time, and it's their way of learning about the world. As they continue to experiment, they build upon existing knowledge like layering a cake.

How Was His Theory Developed?

How does someone come up with an in-depth theory based on a child's mind? Jean Piaget started out as your average male. He was born in Switzerland in the late 1900s, and he was always an eager student. When he was just 11 years old, he published his first scientific paper. Not so average anymore, is he? His drive to learn at a young age could be what influenced him to study children's minds when he grew up.

Jean Piaget was introduced to the development of children's minds when he worked as an assistant to Alfred Binet and Theodore Simon, scientists who developed the standard IQ test. This, combined with his own observations of his daughter and nephew, led him to take an interest in human cognition. Many people at that time thought that children's brains were just mini versions of adult brains, but as Piaget studied, he was led to believe that knowledge was actually learned and acquired throughout different stages.

Piaget watched as young children and older children played. He noticed the difference in what they would do, and he believed that a three-year-old was much different developmentally than an eight-year-old. With this in mind, he developed his four stages of cognitive development.

What cognitive development refers to is the change in cognitive processes and abilities over time. Piaget believed that early cognitive development relied mostly on actions, and this would later change to mental operations. The four stages that he believed in and came up with are presented below.

The Sensorimotor Stage[vii]

This is the first stage of Piaget's theory, and it extends from when a child is born to when they are two years old. Obviously, a newborn knows next to nothing when they are born, but the first two years of life are crucial to a child's development. When they are first born, infants only know the world through their movements and sensations. This is why some babies love to play with different textures and pull on shirts, hair, or grasp blankets in their hands. Everything they touch is a new experience. Their sucking reflex, either from the breast or bottle, is an important developmental skill.

Over the next few months, infants will learn object permanence. If you hide an object from a baby, they will think it disappeared if they are young enough. However, once they are a bit older, they know your ice cream cone didn't disappear behind your back. Their minds have processed that the ice cream cone is still alive and well.

Another important skill they learn is that they are separate from other people, and they learn that their actions cause things to happen. Pressing a button on a toy could make it sing, touching a ball will make it roll, and pulling on mom's hair might just elicit a scream. These first two years are by far the most dramatic when it comes to how much they learn and grow. A two-year-old is wildly different than a newborn.

Infants and toddlers focus on their sensory experiences and developing motor skills. Every time they interact with their environment, they learn more about it. If we all learned at the same rate as infants and toddlers do in their first two years, we wouldn't have a problem learning all languages, becoming Olympic athletes overnight, and uncovering the mysteries of science.

Children go from not being able to hold their heads up to walking and talking by age two. Their language skills are acquired from everyone surrounding them, and they learn a great deal from the caregivers they interact with. This stage is so important that Piaget actually broke it down into subgroups which talk about specific things learned during that time period. Those subgroups are:

- Reflexes: Coming out of the womb requires some changes to be made, and babies learn important reflexes like using their eyes to look around and the sucking reflex used to sustain themselves through eating.

- Primary Circular Reactions: From months one to four, infants accidentally do an action, but then repeat it. For example, the first time sucking on their thumb might be an accident, but they'll do it again because they found it to be soothing for them. It's their way of coping and figuring out how to really use their body.

- Secondary Circular Reactions: Big growth happens from months four to eight because they learn to do an action for a response. This includes grabbing toys to chew on, or grabbing and playing with soft objects.

- Coordination of Reactions: Between eight and 12 months, children learn to explore a lot more of their environment. They'll start imitating their parents and siblings, and they can put two and two together. For example, a child might know that when they press a button on a certain toy that it is going to start singing.

- Tertiary Circular Reactions: The months get longer, and this stage goes from one year to 18 months. This is when they begin their small experimentations, like when they scream that high-pitched scream because they know it gets attention from their parents.

- Early Representational Thought: Between the latter half of one to two, between 18-24 months, children start thinking more and understanding the world in their mind rather than just through their actions. This developmental stage seems to happen overnight, and parents will wake up one day to a baby who talks!

The Preoperational Stage[viii]

Between the ages of two and seven years old, kids begin to learn more words, associate these words with pictures, and they can think symbolically. However, this age range is also very egocentric, which means that they think about themselves and cannot view situations from other people's perspectives. That's why children who argue and don't want to share with each other quite literally cannot understand *why* they would have to share. It doesn't make sense to them at this point in development.

How Piaget found this out was running an experiment he called "the three mountain task." A child would look at a mountain and then was asked later what they saw with some mountain pictures. The children would correctly identify their own viewpoint of the mountain every time.

However, when researchers asked what someone else on the other side of the mountain would see, the children would still choose their same viewpoint.

The problem with this task was that it was a bit difficult for children to understand. Some questioned this egocentric point of view of children because when the experiment was run with different items, like dolls instead of mountains, they could correctly identify what the viewpoint of someone else would be. While children at this age are certainly egocentric, they may be able to understand another person's point of view earlier than the seven years old that Piaget had thought.

Children in this stage still think in concrete terms, though they are getting better with their language and thinking. This is why if a pet dies and you say something like "He went to a farm over the Rainbow Bridge." the child is going to quite literally think there is a farm with a rainbow bridge that's holding their beloved Fido.

Language started in the sensorimotor stage, but this is where it really shines. While a child can say a few different words before the age of two, at this age they'll start stringing together ideas and sentences. Dolls and plastic animals become real, and their pretend play emerges as they talk to their toys. It's an important developmental milestone in this age, which is why play time is so important to kids. They might dress up and play princess, play house as a mommy or daddy, or even role-play as doctors and teachers. Whatever they see in the world around them comes out in this pretend play time. It's like it is their way of seeing the world and analyzing it. While they might not understand different people's perspectives, they can pretend play from these perspectives. Piaget believed that this pretend play is what would set them up for empathizing in the next stage.

One thing that children at this stage struggle with is an idea called "constancy." If I have two different glasses, one wide and one tall, but I pour a cup of water into both containers, which container has more water? For adults, we want to laugh at this question. Obviously, the containers have the same amount of water. You just watched me pour exactly one cup of water into both containers. However, for children in the preoperational stage, they'll most likely choose whatever container they think is larger. Some children will pick the tall glass because the line of water is taller than the line of water in the wide bowl. Some kids might choose the wide bowl because it looks bigger than the tall and skinny glass. The key here is that they don't understand that these two glasses are holding the same amount of water.

The Concrete Operational Stage[ix]

From ages seven to 11, children start to think a lot more logically about events that happen to them. Unlike the children in past stages, these children will understand that one cup of water is still one cup of water, whether or not it was poured into a tall or wide glass. They are more organized, but they still think in very concrete terms. These children will have a hard time understanding abstract ideas or thoughts. Another development is that they begin to use what is called "inductive logic." This is just reasoning from information to form a principle, such as if they get in trouble for lying, then they can draw the conclusion that lying is bad.

This is important because their egocentric personalities start to dissolve at this point. They can understand how another person is feeling when they get into an argument, and they can also see how their best friend may not have been able to kick the goal in during soccer, even though from their own perspective it seemed clear. It helps set them up for life because understanding and empathizing with others' perspectives is an essential skill.

Building off that idea, kids in the concrete operational stage can also identify that their thoughts are separate from their families' and friends' thoughts. For example, just because Sam hates Brussels sprouts doesn't mean that Sam's friend Marla hates Brussels sprouts. Sam can understand that it's okay for Marla to like Brussels sprouts despite the fact that he hates them. He can also realize that throwing Marla's

Brussels sprouts on the ground might hurt Marla's feelings.

The logic in this age range is purely inductive, which means that kids still have a hard time with ideas that don't make sense. For example, a child might notice that every time they are around their friend's dog, they feel sick. They might go home and tell their mom that they're allergic to dogs because they get sick around them. However, the same child might not understand a math problem like, "John has three cookies. Suzy also has three cookies. Jenna has the same amount of cookies as Suzy. How many cookies do John and Jenna each have?" While the answer is obviously a variant of A=B and B=C, these children can't understand that A=C as well.

Children in this stage can also practice reversibility. What this means is that a child can work backward. A child can realize that their fish is a guppy, that a guppy is a fish, and that a fish is an animal. Their thoughts take on more meaning, and they develop a lot in this area.

Children of this stage still do not understand anything abstract. While they can understand different parts of a problem, their thinking is still focused on solely logical thoughts. Anything abstract just goes over their head when it is mentioned, and it might even frustrate them because they don't understand it.

The Formal Operational Stage[x]

This is the last stage of Piaget's theory, and it runs from 12 years through adulthood. The main component of this stage is that children can finally learn to think in abstract terms. Thinking and reasoning over hypothetical problems or questions will no longer cause concern or frustration. Their abstract thought finally emerges. When they get into adolescence, they'll start to think more about moral, philosophical, political, social, and ethical issues. All of these topics require abstract thought, and it is only in this stage that it emerges. Deductive logic finally emerges, which means that they can use reasoning from a principle to identify specific information.

There were two different ways Piaget came to his conclusions on when abstract thought emerges. One experiment took place with the use of weights. The distance of the weights, as well as the weight itself, would affect the scale. Children of all ages were tasked with balancing the scale. While some children would get it with trial and error, it wasn't until the age of 13 that children could create a hypothesis of where to put each weight for it to be balanced.

Another experiment involved asking where someone would put a third eye. Lots of the younger kids would say that they would put an eye in the middle of their forehead. It seemed like an easy answer to them, but the older children were smarter in their responses. What use is a third eye if it is already near where your other eyes are? The teens all responded with better alternatives like the middle of the hand to look ahead when you can't see, or on the back of the head, to see what's going on behind them. While these answers may seem silly and not at all scientific, it showed that these older kids could think much more abstractly than the younger children.

Another important characteristic that emerges at this age is problem-solving. While most kids could already solve problems before this age, it was based on trial and error. For example, they may know that taking June's jump rope makes her sad, so the next time they're at recess, they don't take her jump rope.

Adolescents in this stage don't need the trial and error. They can think about the problem systematically, and they'll come to the conclusion before they do it. That doesn't mean they won't still hurt people's feelings, because hey, we all do it. But simple concepts like what happens when you steal someone's belongings don't have to be learned via trial and error. They already know that June won't want her jump rope stolen because *they* wouldn't want their jump rope stolen.

Metacognition is also developed in this stage of Piaget's theory. This is what happens when you think about your thoughts. Trippy, right? But we do it all the time. We daydream, we question our daydream, we wonder why our minds are thinking this, we try to shut it off, and it's a daily occurrence whether or not you know it. Metacognition is very important in adulthood, and it is directly tied to abstract thinking.

By the time children enter the formal operational stage, they are utilizing their problem-solving skills as second nature. Children in this final stage of development use critical thinking skills to think back on how to solve problems in order to find solutions.[xi]

Perhaps one of the most interesting things about Piaget's theory is that he didn't believe that intellectual development was quantitative. We don't just gather knowledge and pile it up in our brains as we get older. Instead, he believed that our development and thinking is much more qualitative. To argue this, he made the point that a two-year-old and a seven-year-old have the same amount of information about the world. What's different is how they see it and think about it. This is inherently a qualitative attribute, and he believed that there was a critical change in how we think about the world as we move through these four stages.

There are some factors that help children learn and grow, and they're important to know before moving through this book.

The first term you need to know is "schemas." A schema defines the mental and physical actions involved in understanding and knowing. They are the organized building blocks of knowledge and help us to understand the world around us. If you didn't have a mental model of your world, you would not be able to use information from your past experience or to plan your future.

Schemas tell us how to react to incoming stimuli or information. When you find out something that invalidates a schema you have, you replace that schema with the new one. Or, when you find out more information about a certain topic, you add more information to the schema you already have.

Let's say that a child loves crunchy carrots. They have a schema in their mind that says that anything that is orange and crunchy is a carrot. However, one day they are introduced to the guilty pleasure of Cheetos. This adds new information to their schema, so they realize that not all orange and crunchy things are carrots.

Their schema now holds more information than it did before.

The second term that Piaget introduced to the world was "assimilation." This is the process of taking in new information into your existing schemas. So when the child believed that everything orange and crunchy was a carrot, they encountered new information when they were introduced to the Cheetos. They have now assimilated the Cheetos into their orange-and-crunchy schema.

"Accommodation" is another term to know, and it is the process of changing and altering schemas when new information is presented to you. This happens when new information or experiences come into your life, like when the child was introduced to what Cheetos are. New schemas can be added during this process as well. So maybe the child created a new schema of orange-and-crunchy chips and orange-and-crunchy vegetables.

Last, but certainly not least, is the term "equilibration." This is when a balance is formed between assimilation and accommodation. It is through this process that equilibration is born. It is the knowledge of when to apply previous known knowledge in your existing schemas and when to change your schemas to add in additional and new knowledge. Equilibration is responsible for how those move from different stages of thought.

Piaget's cognitive development theory helped us to understand the intellectual growth that happens between when a child is born and the remainder of their childhood years. He was the first to suggest that humans are not passive in their knowledge. Instead, from the time we are born, humans are constantly running experiments and investigating to understand how everything around them works. At the same time, we could see that we adopt some schemas—and once they are ingrained enough, we are prone to function on autopilot. Making decisions on autopilot can often lead to undesired outcomes. While our critical thinking skills start to develop as early as two years old, thinking critically with intention requires a certain age and maturity.

I presented Piaget's theory with the hope to illustrate how human cognition develops from birth, and why it is safe to assume that some thinking patterns are mechanical—and so they need to be questioned. In the next chapters we'll learn practical examples about how to do this questioning.

Chapter 3: What Are the Main Guidelines of Critical Thinking?

Based on the guidelines established by Wade & Tavris in their books, *Psychology* (5th edition, Longman Publishers, 1998) and *Psychology in Perspective* (2nd edition, Longman, 1997), I've elaborated on the seven main steps of critical thinking.

1. The first step to start thinking critically is learning to ask good questions.

Allow yourself to wonder and reflect on your questions—and the answers given to them. Seek out questions that have not been answered yet. Look for the ignored parts in an argument.

- Why is it ignored?
- How did this problem end up looking like this?
- What's wrong here?
- Why is it like this and not like that?

A story:

People often decide to make changes in their daily lives based on other people's anecdotes. For example, some people are convinced if they take a vitamin C supplement every day, they will stay healthy. Why? At some point in their life, someone important like their mother or a good friend told them so.

My friend was sold this belief, too. We used to travel often and it was difficult to keep up with our daily routines. Once, he ran out of his vitamin C supplements and couldn't buy new ones for a few days. And in these few days he caught a cold. He insisted that if he had taken his vitamin C dose every day, he wouldn't have developed the cold. Now, many people hearing his story and reasoning would just accept it and think "Vitamin C keeps you from getting a cold. You see, faithless Zoe, he didn't have the vitamin C, so he got sick."

This type of cause-and-effect thinking lacks critical thinking skills. However, it is the most common way of thinking. If X happens, Y follows.

Let's examine this story a little more closely. The first information vacuum is that we don't have real evidence to support the idea that vitamin C prevents illness. My friend's mother's opinion as proof is hardly enough. Why vitamin C, anyway? Why not vitamin A, or any other vitamin? The first step is to discover real evidence of whether or not vitamin C helps your immune system to be more resistant against colds.

The next step is to analyze my friend's specific case. Even if it turns out that vitamin C helps to prevent colds, it doesn't mean that there was a direct link between him not taking his vitamins and getting the cold. It sounds fair to think that, but is it really?

We were traveling, exposed to a totally unfamiliar environment—new climate, new food. There is no evidence proving he wouldn't have gotten a cold even if he took his vitamin C.

Based on two studies published in Harvard Health Publishing there is little evidence vitamin C is helpful towards preventing colds, but if taken regularly, it can diminish the impact of cold symptoms.[xii]

2. Properly articulate the questions to define the problem.

When you get an idea of what may be wrong in an argument, think about how to phrase your questions. Sometimes an improperly formulated question can lead to partial or defensive answers. Keep your questions neutral. People don't like to be proven wrong, so don't be obvious with your questions. Make sure to not influence with your questions. (Unless that's your goal. But that's not critical thinking, that's manipulation.) If you ask a question that presupposes an answer, you won't get the objective picture.

A story:

There are times when people abuse critical thinking skills (or the lack of them) and use questioning for the purpose of manipulation.

Politicians, for instance, can influence the future of an entire country when they phrase questions that suggest a clear answer.

A classic story about manipulative questioning is the "four-part referendum" in Hungary. The referendum was held on 26 November 1989 after the collapse of the communist regime in that country. The four questions the voters were asked were the following:

- Should the president be elected after parliamentary elections?

- Should the Hungarian Socialist Workers' Party be banned from workplaces?

- Should the Hungarian Socialist Workers' Party account for its properties owned or managed by it?

- Should the Workers' Militia be dissolved?

The referendum was elicited by the joint effort of the Hungarian right-wing parties to try to postpone the presidential elections until after the parliamentary elections.

Why?

Because before parliamentary elections, the president would have been elected with direct election (people electing the president by voting), and thus the then-popular Secretary of State, Imre Pozsgay, member of the old communist party, would have won. Three questions of the referendum were obvious "yes" answers. Among these questions, the catch was hidden—the first question. Many people—as expected—just ticked yes—yes—yes—yes on the referendum.

As a consequence, the presidential elections were postponed until after the parliamentary election. Thus the first democratic parliament could quickly pass a law that appointed parliament to elect the president instead of the misled populous.

As you can see, some critical thinking skills could have helped Hungarians see through the scheme of their resourceful right-wing party. Regardless of how good or bad the consequence of this referendum proved to be, one thing remains true: the population got deceived.

So how do you ask good questions related to a problem?

The first and simplest question we should ask when it comes to a problem is: "Why is this a problem?" Answering this question we will often discover that the problem is not even the real problem, just a symptom of it. The deeper we dig, the more often we ask this "Why is this a problem?" question, the better we'll understand what the actual, real problem is.

When the "problem" is a person's opinion, it's smart to approach the conversation with some tact. This means staying away from blaming language and focusing on the problem—which is the person's opinion, not the person itself. It can help if we say what we want to say as a reference about our emotions or thoughts. So for example, instead of saying, "You are wrong when you say this..." try "I feel XYZ way about this topic but I'm curious to understand why you think that. Can you elaborate?"

Being tactful when using critical inquiry can help us get to the information we need quicker than if we use critical inquiry elephant style. People are much more likely to open up when they are not put on their defenses.

3. Examine the evidence and look for assumptions and biases.

Think about what evidence supports or refutes the argument in question. Just because many people believe in something—including people who seem knowledgeable about the topic—doesn't make it automatically true. All of us are susceptible to biases. Our emotions prevent us from being impartial. When you evaluate the biases behind arguments, don't forget to check your own.

A story:

The most illustrative way to present biases in correlation with critical thinking is to talk about cognitive biases. Let's take a popular one, confirmation bias. Why do we always think we're right?

Warren Buffet once said, "What the human being is best at doing is interpreting all new information so that their prior conclusions remain intact." What does this mean?

People are wired to look at new information from an angle to confirm their theories rather than to contradict or test them. When something disproves their theories, they tend to have an emotional reaction or simply ignore the disproval. And when I say they, I mean me—and you. All of us. We do this by default. Only by paying attention and questioning our gut reactions can we defeat them.

Why is confirmation bias our default answer? For the same reason we tend to accept others' opinions without question. It's easier, and we seek quick and easy explanations. It takes less energy to keep our worldview intact, rather than to question and often rewrite it.

But we want to become critical thinkers. Critical thinking is not fast thinking. It depends on the accurate processing of new and existing information to provide an answer to the actual situation. Confirmation bias can easily cause confusion and inaccurate results, if you're not careful.

The good news is that confirmation bias is easily detectable, once you know to look for it. Now, after reading these lines, you have no excuse. You know. There is a good little exercise to improve your confirmation bias detector: purposely attempt to deconstruct and question your own thoughts simply to compensate for your natural tendency to support them.

What do you need to do more, exactly?

Choose a theory you really like and decide it is the unquestionable truth. Got it? Now spend half an hour on the internet looking for proof that disproves this theory. Chances are that you'll find approving material first—don't give up. Almost everything has a pro and con. When you find disproving data—even if you don't accept it—just think about why that person says what they say or believes what they believe.

For example, I used to be very close-minded when it came to infidelity. I thought if someone cheated, that was the end. Nothing could be said or done to make it right. There are some people out there who don't share my view, who can and are able to accept infidelity, forgive and move on and be happy. I found success stories of couples who recovered from cheating. I don't need to read too deep into the book *Sapiens* to find that only in a minority of human existence is monogamy the norm.

Even though I had my strict views on infidelity, the opposite view can also work. There are situations when there is only one correct answer. Take the Scramble Squares puzzle, for instance. It has only one good arrangement, but more than 95 billion possibilities ($4^9 * 9!$). Whatever your random choice was, based on the big numbers' chances, it might not be as correct as you think.

4. Avoid emotional reasoning.

Just because you feel a certain way, it doesn't mean you're right. Remember my example of cheating—just because I think cheating is unforgivable, it doesn't mean it is really so.

The recent hype around trusting your gut enables many people to passionately commit to a view without thinking clearly about it. More often than not, results are not as pleasing as the "I will never die" gut feeling that caused the problem.

People who actively engage in emotional reasoning tend to think that what they feel is right—sometimes even against disproving evidence. They are prone to mix up their feelings with facts. Feelings are subjective. They might not always reflect the big-picture (external) reality.

Most commonly and ironically, an external event triggers emotional reasoning.

A story:

After losing a loved one, did you ever start explaining natural phenomena as a sign or presence? Let's say a cloud looked like the chair of your recently passed away grandma, or that rain started to pour on you right after you broke up with someone and you thought that even the sky was crying for you. Right? These things happen fairly often.

This kind of belief can take more extreme forms. For example, when you decide the time has come to do something dangerous just because the tile fell two inches away from your head and you associate this miracle with something like being a chosen one for something extreme.

There are internally triggered emotional reasonings too. Some people are prone to manufacturing stories in their heads without much input from the external world. They are very reactive to the current feelings they have, regardless of whether or not there's a basis for that feeling in reality. Have you ever felt like something bad was happening and you called your mom, your spouse, or kid and asked if everything was okay? And even after you got the confirmation, you swung restlessly in front of your computer, checking for accidents and sudden tornadoes or plane crashes?

That being said, emotional reasoning is not a bad thing. Correctly combined and balanced with critical thinking, it can be quite beneficial. Certain emotions like compassion, empathy, the ability to read others, and being sensitive to the feelings of others are very important in making our critical reasoning right. We don't want to hurt others with our critical thinking. In fact, research presented by Harvard Business Review shows that managers who use both IQ and emotional reasoning are much more successful than those who operate with raw facts, ignoring the human factor.[xiii]

5. Avoid overgeneralizations.

Generalization's big brother, overgeneralization, can bite our critical thinking endeavors in the leg if we're not careful. We overgeneralize when we extend the features of a few elements from a group more than is reasonable. This way we arrive to broad and inaccurate conclusions.

A story:

Let's take a look at generalization. It is the process of extending the attributives of a few elements from a group to the entire group. It doesn't matter what we analyze, when we come in contact with one or a few elements of a group, we notice some common characteristics. By generalizing, we automatically conclude that each element of the group shares the same characteristics.

Theoretically speaking, we have a group. Let's call it group A. We notice that member A1 has attributive X. Member A2 has the same attributive X. So does member A3. By knowing the attributives of A1, A2, and A3, and generalizing, we extend our conclusion to the entire group. This means to A4, A5, and all the way to A100.

Generalization, if used correctly, can be quite helpful in scientific fields. It speeds up research and helps to make conclusions of an entire group without analyzing each individual member. For example, if you see a group of bulls on a field and they have horns, it is safe to say that generally, bulls have horns.

The problem with overgeneralization.

Let's see two typical examples of overgeneralization.

1. You meet two students from Harvard University, and you have the impression that they are unkind. If you start chanting, "All people at Harvard are unkind," you've overgeneralized.

What's the problem with this?

First, you generalized from a small sample (two people) about an entire group. You can take the generalization to even bigger groups, like thinking that all educated people are unkind, just because two happened to be.

2. You want to research the coffee-drinking preferences of coffee lovers. So you go to each specialty café in Seattle and ask about the coffee preferences of the people drinking coffee there.

After you've collected the data, you generalize that coffee-lovers like this and that type of coffee, prepared in a certain way.

What's wrong with this overgeneralization?

Even though you analyzed a bigger sample (each coffee shop in Seattle), you can't apply your results to the entire world. Coffee lovers in Seattle may be different than coffee lovers in Vietnam or Colombia. Generalizing from a large but unrepresentative sample and applying that generalization to the entire population is just as incorrect as generalizing from a small sample.

The helpful generalization, in this case, would have been to conclude on the collective coffee-drinking habits of the people of Seattle only.

In real life we overgeneralize way too often. As I pointed out before, our brain prefers quick and easy explanations. But it is hungry for knowledge and certainty. The mish-mash of these two cravings (quick solution and hunger for knowledge) is overgeneralization. We make broad conclusions about our surroundings based on little experience or data. Add our natural tendency to think negatively to the equation and the recipe for anxiety and stress is ready.

The antidote to overgeneralization is objective self-analysis and thought assessment. Start paying attention to the ideas and convictions you have about the world and yourself. Observe which of your ideas are overly simplified or generalized.

When you catch yourself overgeneralizing, the next step to take is to question its validity. Ask questions about the quantity or quality of empirical data experiences that support it. Let's say you got a new neighbor who was very loud in the first week after they moved in. This understandably bothered you. Ask yourself these questions before jumping to the conclusion that your neighbor is a party animal:

- How do I know this?
- What's the real-life evidence that proves this?
- Is this proof really relevant enough?

If your neighbor was loud once at night, that is not enough reason to think "They are a loud party animal, let's move to the other side of the country." or "I should call the police, let's take them out of the neighborhood." If, however, the neighbor parties each night like there's no tomorrow, it is sensible to go and talk to them about the noise.

Let's say your neighbor was not a party animal—they just had a housewarming party once. So you got settled on the idea that they are not that loud generally. Unfortunately, your work is not done here. Your mind might wander back to the old, overgeneralizing assumptions whenever your neighbor becomes louder than mute. This is why maybe the most important step in controlling overgeneralizing is to keep questioning your assumptions over and over. The more you do it, the less strongly the symptoms of overgeneralization will arise.

The last step for overcoming overgeneralization is taking action to gain real experience and evidence. In our case, get to know your neighbor. See for yourself what kind of person they are, why they're loud, and so on. This experience will help you gain a more realistic picture about the situation, and make better conclusions or decisions about it.

Look for real-life proof before generalizing. The proof has to be relevant, recent, and frequent enough.

6. Consider other interpretations.

Resist the urge to jump to premature conclusions when you have only a little evidence. Even when you gather sufficient evidence, look for other events, explanations, or behaviors that could still be considered before drawing a conclusion. Minimize the amount of assumptions in the explanation.

A story:

Take a look at the picture above. What do you
see? A young woman or an old woman?
Whatever you saw, you were right. Now try and

see the other version. If you saw the old woman first, try to make out the young woman, and vice versa. This optical illusion represents well how we should approach the sixth aspect of critical thinking, namely considering other interpretations.

Considering others' or other interpretations can not only lead you to a more accurate answer but it can also help you understand who people really are. Let's consider the following example: Mary and Luke have been dating for a few months when Luke decided to surprise Mary with an afternoon doing their shared hobby, tennis. They have been talking about how much they loved playing tennis for weeks, how they both learned the game in infancy, and how it was the best family pastime of their childhood. They both stepped excited onto the tennis court. An hour later they came off the field annoyed at each other, and they were close to having their very first fight. What happened?

Mary was more upfront with her feelings so she spoke up. "I don't understand. I felt you were letting me win this entire time. You should have put yourself to the task and play like your life depended on it!"

Luke was confused. "My life depended on it? It's just a game. I came here to relax and play."

It turns out that while playing tennis was an important game in both of their lives, Mary and Luke had totally different interpretations on what it means to play tennis for fun. Mary grew up in a competitive family where playing tennis was all about winning. Everybody in her family tried their best while they played, and they liked it that way. If someone was not giving their best, it was a sign of disrespect—"You allowed me to win because you think I'm not good enough."

For Luke, playing tennis meant going to the court, pass a ball back and forth, goof around, be chill, sometimes follow the rules, sometimes not… To him, tennis was all about relaxed family time. If someone became competitive, it was considered a bit of a douchebag cliché, in Luke's experience.

Had they talked about how they were raised on the tennis court, they might have avoided this clash. Luckily, they understood that they had totally different interpretations of the same thing and that there was nothing wrong with either, so they reached a compromise: one chill game, and one at their best. They ended up enjoying both.

This is why it is important to get a wide variety of information and experience before jumping to a conclusion. Had Mary concluded that Luke was looking down on her, or had Luke thought that all Mary wanted was to defeat him, they might have developed resentment and anger towards each other. Partial or incomplete information can lead to partial, incomplete, premature, or incorrect answers.

There is an anecdote about blind people meeting with an elephant for the first time. One touches the ears and thinks the elephant is some kind of fan. One touches the tail and says it's like a rope. Another holds the trunk of the elephant and is convinced it is a big snake. Some hold the legs, thinking they are moving trees. They are all right, considering their perspective, but only together can they have the correct answer. Only by touching each part of the elephant.

How to avoid projection bias?

Getting familiar with other interpretations can help us with our tendency to project our worldview onto others. As individuals, we live in our own heads all the time. It is difficult to think outside our own box. Projection bias means that often we tend to assume that others think just like us—thus, we don't even search for alternative information.

Even though there may be no proof of it, we end up thinking that others think like us and agree with us. And when they don't... that's when we get confused, offended, bitter, or resentful. We end up thinking that the person in question misled us when the only misleading factor was our own mind.

Stay open to others' interpretations. Ask questions and let in opposing information. Your mind, however smart it may be, is just one mind. Sharing its content with others can only broaden your knowledge and your critical judgment accuracy.

7. Tolerate uncertainty.

Critical thinking doesn't guarantee you an answer for everything. Sometimes the best you can get is an "I don't know." And that's fine. There is no capital-letter Answer for everything. Sometimes there is no right answer, or the evidence merely allows getting to experimental conclusions that shouldn't be taken for granted.

There are some natural uncertainties in life—like our future. Unless you believe in tarot cards and fortune-tellers, our future is always surrounded with uncertainty. Being anxious about it from time to time is normal. Everybody has a different level of tolerance to uncertainty.

A story:

Being uncomfortable with uncertainty is normal, to a certain degree. The problem occurs when someone is intolerant to uncertainty. What do you think? Can you tolerate uncertainties?

If you find yourself doing more of the things mentioned below, chances are you have room for improvement at tolerating uncertainty:

- Do you seek constant reassurance from others? Do you ask your partner each day if they love you? Do you photo message your friend about your outfit before you go on a date? Do you call your mom before buying something for the kitchen?

- Are you a neurotic list-maker? Some people feel better and more certain about their future if they list everything on paper. They need step-by-step guides to business, groceries, morning routines, evening routines, dog feeding routines... You get it.

- Are you a notorious double-checker? Do you reread your texts before sending them? Do you call your loved ones multiple times a day to make sure everything is okay? Do you double-check meeting dates, your makeup, your credit card balance—hourly?

- Is "work's the best done if it is done by me" your mantra? People who have an issue tolerating uncertainty don't like to leave tasks in the hands of others because they can't be sure the work will end up as they expect it. They do the chores, the presentation, and they take the kid to school. Just to be sure.

- The ultimate busy-man. Some people try to distract themselves from their anxieties caused by uncertainty by keeping themselves busy. If they don't have the time to think, they feel more relieved.

- Excessive procrastination is another sign of uncertainty intolerance. He who doesn't work won't make working errors, right?

So, are you intolerant to uncertainty? Relax, my friend. We all are, to some degree. There is no way you can eradicate uncertainty from your life. The only thing you can do is raise your level of tolerance. How?

First of all, analyze what the exact patterns are in your life that indicate you are intolerant to uncertainty. What makes you anxious? Write them down. Now rate them on a scale of 1 to 10, 10 being very anxious, 1 being anxious only a tiny bit.

Got them? Now write them down again—according to your rating. On the top of your paper should be the thing that makes you *the least* anxious, followed by the things that make you progressively more anxious.

Now practice tolerance. Start with the first item on your list. Maybe it's "Did I feed the cat?" Come on. It is a fat cat, they'll survive until morning. There is no need to debate for half an hour at half past midnight whether or not you should feed them again. Resist the urge to get up.

When you feel comfortable about your cat's nutrition, go to the next uncertainty. Should I call my friend about the outfit I'm wearing to the party? Nope. For once, just decide it for yourself. There will be no catastrophe, even if you show up in something your friend wouldn't approve of. I'm not saying you should never ask your friend about your outfit. This is an exercise with little to no risk to learn to tolerate uncertainty more.

Why do I say this? Because there are uncertainties with higher risk factors—the ones you have with number 10 on your list. You can't start your tolerance learning curve on those ones because, before you know it, you'll crawl back under your blanket and watch Netflix forever. Start small. Practice tolerance with the low-risk events. Go to a movie without reading the review. Buy a cheap shirt without trying it on. Tell a joke without thinking it through 100 times. Ask a stranger what time it is.

Follow up on your progress. Ask these critical evaluation questions:

- Did things turn out well, even though you were not totally certain?—If not:
- What happened?—Be objective.
- Were you able to handle the negative outcome?
    - If yes: What did you do to cope with the negative outcome?
    - If not: What could you have done differently to cope with the negative outcome?
- What does this tell you about your coping ability with negative outcomes in the future?

Sometimes things work out as planned, sometimes they don't. There is a fifty-fifty chance: yes or no. You can't do much about it;

this is the nature of the beast. The best you can do is strengthen your tolerance, improve your reactions to the undesired outcome, and stay critical-minded.

Chapter 4: The Science of Paul-Elder

Did you know that thinking could cost you? It is an interesting concept, but if your thinking is peppered with lots of biases and you're prone to over-think, you're costing yourself time, effort, and money. Have you ever thought too long on something, and by the time you were ready to commit, it was gone? Or maybe you didn't know what to do, so you made a split-second decision and it turned out to be a bad one? Any time you are thinking hastily, you are risking changing the quality of your life. And as much as I wish I could say it was for the better, often it isn't.

We're all a bit egocentric, which means we love to think about ourselves. I mean, we're living in our own bodies, so it makes sense to be a little selfish. And if you're already a little selfish, let me tell you why you could excel at critical thinking.

Critical thinking is all up to *you.* No one can force you to think critically, and anyone who thinks critically isn't going to want to spend the time to beg you to do it. Critical thinking is completely self-directed. You decide when you want to do it, you decide whether or not you are even going to do it, and it can be hard to keep that mindfulness when you're starting out. However, it is so worth it. The benefits far outweigh the costs to you.

The substantive approach developed by Dr. Richard Paul and his colleagues was developed over multiple decades. It is celebrated because it can be used in almost every subject, discipline, and profession. It is by far one of the best, and it contains five essential dimensions, which are analysis, assessment, dispositions, skill and abilities, and obstacles or barriers. I'll talk more about the standards and everything else about this approach as this chapter continues.

Universal Intellectual Standards[xiv]

First of all, it starts with universal intellectual standards. These are the standards that should be applied every time you think about the quality of your reasoning. These are used whenever you have a problem or situation on your hands.

Clarity

If someone says something that doesn't make sense, we can't decide whether or not it is true. We don't even know if it is relevant to the situation at hand because we can't understand it. This happens when we get asked vague questions where we don't understand what the problem is. Whoever is presenting the situation has a view of the problem that we don't know as intimately as them, so it is confusing if they keep things in vague terms. If you are unsure what someone is saying, try asking them, "Could you give me an example?" It's a polite way to get them to open up about what they are trying to say.

Accuracy

People say things that are clear all the time, but many times they are not accurate. Someone could say, "Most cheetahs have blue spots." We understand what they are saying, but it isn't correct. Try asking the person, "How could we verify or test that?"

Precision

How often are people super vague with what they say? People can be clear, accurate, and not at all precise. It's like when someone says, "The ocean is deep." Yes, yes it is, but *how deep?* Try asking the person, "Could you be more specific?"

Relevance

Can you believe that things can be clear, accurate, precise, but not relevant? Someone could be saying, "As you can see, Jerry has gained about 50 pounds." Well, that's great, but why are you talking about Jerry's weight gain during a business meeting? When these things come up, ask, "How does that help us with the issue?"

Depth

Depth issues happen when serious things are dealt with using non-serious solutions. While everything about the solution might be relevant, precise, accurate, and clear, it might lack that "oomph" factor. The depth. The statement "Practice safe sex," which is used in a lot of sex education lectures, lacks depth. Unsafe sex practices could lead to lifelong infections, so there should be a little more depth than just telling the person to practice safe sex. Try asking yourself and others when presented with an issue something like, "What are some of the difficulties or threats we need to consider?"

Breadth

Breadth issues happen when you don't try to see multiple viewpoints. You can have the best solution in the world, but if it is solely one-sided, it isn't going to work or wow anyone that you are close with. Try asking, "Do we need to consider another point of view?" Most often, you'll find the answer to that question is yes.

Logic

Thoughts get combined into logic, but sometimes our thinking isn't as logical as we think it is. If your combination of different thoughts is not making sense, then your combination isn't as logical as you had hoped. Sometimes, things just sound confusing. So ask yourself, "Does all of this make sense together?"

Significance

Are you really focusing on the right problem? Sometimes we find ourselves caught up in something that isn't even truly a problem. If you are questioning whether or not you are solving the most significant problem, you probably aren't. Try asking, "Is this the central idea to focus on?"

Fairness

We all struggle with being fair. From our own declarations of "Life's not fair!" to the declarations of "You're so unfair!" we love to talk about fairness. However, we don't think of our own wants and needs at the same level we think of everyone else's wants and needs. We tend to think we're a bit more important.

Still, we have to *try* to keep things fair. Work hard at applying fairness to everything you do. Even if you think that you are being fair, question yourself. Try asking, "Am I taking into account the thinking of others? Am I distorting things to get what I want?"

The Elements of Thinking[xv]

Dr. Richard Paul and Dr. Linda Elder identified the intellectual standards that need to be known in order to identify the elements of thinking. I just talked to you about the standards, and here are the elements:

Purpose

Let's say you're doing a project with others about cleaning up trash in the ocean. What would your purpose be? Most likely, your purpose would be something like saving the animals in the ocean, or keeping the ocean clean. Did you know that all reasoning has a purpose? Your purpose can be thought of like your goal or objective. It's what you're trying to accomplish, and it's the reason for your motives and functions. It is by far one of the most important elements, but you need to know how to be clear in your purpose. You need to think about your purpose. Your purpose has to be justifiable. You can ask yourself "What is the objective of this project?" or "What is my central aim on this?" These questions can help you find what your purpose is.

Question

Your reasoning is attempting to figure something out and settle a question so that you can solve a problem. You should always state your question. The question lays out what the problem is, and it helps you direct your line of thought to be distinct and clear. If your question is vague, you'll find that your thinking is going to lack clarity. You need to make sure that your question is precise. Your question for the ocean trash cleanup could be something like "Would cleaning up the trash in the ocean help animals to thrive and survive better than they are currently surviving with the trash?" To analyze your question, ask "Is there a better way to put the question?" or "Can I explain my question if someone says they can't understand it?"

Assumptions

Then you need to check what your assumptions are. Reasoning is based on assumptions, so they need to be clear and justified with evidence you have collected. Oftentimes, assumptions can be considered to be beliefs you take for granted that operate in your subconscious, so you're not readily making them and thinking about them. If you need to ask some questions about your assumptions, try "Am I assuming something I shouldn't?" or "What is being assumed in this situation?" If you are doing the ocean cleanup problem, you're assuming that there is trash in the ocean that is harming the animals. Is there truly? This is when you would need to analyze your assumptions.

Point of View

Everyone who reasons is doing it from some point of view. It's nearly impossible to remain objective, and you'll usually approach things from your individual perspective. Looking at things only from the way you see them isn't necessarily bad, but it can come with a lot of limitations. Perhaps your point of view is that trash in the ocean is bad, and anyone who throws out trash and doesn't find a way to recycle or compost is lazy or uneducated about the harm they are doing. However, do you think this is everyone's point of view? No, it probably isn't. You should consider other relevant viewpoints when presented with a situation. To make sure you are remaining as objective as you can, try asking "Is there another way to look at this that I should be considering?" or "Is my view the only reasonable view?" Remember, there are multiple paths up the same mountain.

Information

Gathering information is something that should be done every time you want to make an important decision or take a strong stance. Evidence helps you figure things out in a fair and better way. However, not all of your evidence needs to show that your views are accurate or correct. The more evidence you collect, the more objective you can become. The information you do gather should be accurate regarding whatever it is that you're presented with, though. If you want to target information, ask yourself "What data is relevant here?" or "Do we need to gather more evidence?" Perhaps you could find studies that show animals are being harmed by the leftover plastic and trash in the ocean. Maybe you'll also find studies showing that animals have adapted to the plastics, and the level of harm is decreasing as the years go on. While the second study wouldn't go along with your point of view, it is still relevant to your issue at hand.

Inferences

You need to keep a watch on what you're inferring in situations. These are the conclusions you come to because your mind is trying to figure something out. In a perfect world, inferences will follow the evidence you have gathered. However, we are often guilty of inferring things without evidence. You need to be certain that you are not inferring anything more than what you have found in your situation. Ask yourself "What conclusions am I coming to?" and "Does our solution necessarily follow from our data?"

If your solution is to help pick up trash that washes up on the shore, that wouldn't necessarily help your problem because it would be the trash that has already made its way through the ocean. You would want to stop the problem before it began, so your conclusion wouldn't make too much sense unless it was something like making recycling more accessible and easier for average people.

Concepts

One thing that we struggle with is keeping our concepts clear. You need to clarify your ideas, theories, or hypotheses that you are using to make sense of things. Try asking yourself these questions to clarify your concept: "I think I have a good theory, but can I explain it more fully?" and "Is my idea causing problems for me or others?"

Implications

Your implications and consequences need to be thought through. These are claims that should come from other truths. Implications will follow from your thoughts, and consequences will follow from your actions. Ask yourself "If I decide to do this, what things might happen?" and "What is likely to happen if we do this versus that?" With the ocean scenario, you would think about what would happen if you made recycling more accessible. Would people really start recycling? Would it help the ocean's trash problem? You have to think about the consequences at hand.[xvi]

Valuable Intellectual Traits[xvii]

This is the third part of the critical thinking system of Dr. Paul and Dr. Elder—the valuable intellectual traits. These traits are the most important part of the whole system, so make sure you are reading through them thoroughly!

Intellectual humility

You know what it means to be humble, and that's really where intellectual humility comes about. How many times have you been in the presence of someone who just rubs you the wrong way? Maybe they always have some comment to make about a situation that they know nothing about, or maybe they always try to "one-up" you by adding in information that they think is more valuable.

A lot of us can be that person when it comes to certain topics. However, it never gets any easier to be around this person. No matter who it is or what the situation is, the people who seem to know it all are the people we don't want to be around. You could say that this person lacks intellectual humility. This trait is about knowing where your knowledge ends. It doesn't mean that you have to sit back and relax while someone spreads incorrect information on a topic you consider yourself an expert in, but realize that your knowledge has limits.

As awesome as it would be, we can't know everything. Even people who seem to know a lot do not know *everything.* When you practice intellectual humility, you keep in mind that there are others who know more than you do about certain topics. Your native egocentrism can get in the way, but when you practice your intellectual humility, you quiet your egocentrism. If you listen to others, you'll find that you can learn a lot more.

Also, this takes into account that you have a bias. Sometimes you'll be prejudiced against certain limitations, your viewpoint might be compromised, and you are deceiving yourself with a load of excuses.

Let's say that you love basketball. There's nothing wrong with loving basketball. But let's say that there is a scandal with a basketball player. It turns out that this basketball player is your absolute favorite, so you believe that you know everything about him. When the scandal comes out that he cheated on his taxes, you'll move through a few different stages. First of all, you're probably going to defend this basketball player even though you don't know him. You'll be like, "No, he would *never* do that. I read last year that he hosted a charity event for orphans. Do you think a man hosting charity events for orphans would cheat on his taxes? No, absolutely not."

However, let's say that the person who told you this news is receiving it firsthand from your favorite basketball player's personal assistant. Do you see how you would be biased here? Because you love this basketball player, you don't want to believe the contradicting information that was presented about him. The man's personal assistant obviously knows a lot more about him than you, someone who just reads news stories on him that play on the halo effect.

You're allowed to question someone's view, but immediately shutting it down and presenting information on why you are right is far from humble. You have to be sure that you are not being pretentious about things when you're in a situation where you want to express your knowledge or opinion. There is a right way to voice how you are feeling, but be humble while you are doing it.

Intellectual courage

When you think of courage, you might think of a strong hero going to face a fire and doing something noble and great and dangerous. I mean, that's what courage is, right? Sure, courage can be going through fire or defeating a dragon to get to the princess, but most of the time, courage is much smaller and quieter.

If you don't think you practice courage every day, you're wrong. Anything that is hard for us requires us to practice courage. However, intellectual courage is more about going into our mind and having the courage to find out what is and isn't true in what you believe. Take, for example, the viewpoints of a child. As a child, you conform to whatever your parents tell you. If they are republicans, you become a republican. If they are democrats, you consider yourself to be a democrat. Even though a small child knows nothing about politics, they still talk to their friends about which party they belong to. A lot of the time, these children will grow up and remain in the same political party. It's because it is how they were raised as a child. For those who like everything their parents raised them with, they'll most likely agree with whatever party their parents are in.

However, when do these children decide to truly commit to a party? They can't be researching politics at such a young age. Let's say the same child grows up and meets someone who becomes close to them. This person has the complete opposite political views. They have some debates and arguments about it, but suddenly that child who is now an adult is confused. Are these really their views? Do they really believe *that* when it comes to taxes, abortion, immigration laws, etc.?

If they start to question their beliefs, they are practicing intellectual courage. It isn't the easiest thing to challenge what you thought you knew, but it is an important step. Even if you have strong negative feelings toward something, you should be able to address them with the other side. You might even figure out that your strong feelings were not as strong as you thought they were.

We owe it to ourselves to practice intellectual courage when it comes to our beliefs and viewpoints. It's not right to just accept what we have been taught. Even though we learned these things, they might not be completely true. The more we practice intellectual courage, the more we will find that there is some truth to other viewpoints. You need courage so that you can be true to yourself.

See why this is called courage? It can be really difficult to believe the same thing as everyone else, only to find out that it isn't what you believe in, after all. It is hard, and it can feel dangerous. It might even feel like you're going to walk through a fire and you're unsure what lies on the other side. If we use our intellectual courage, we will be more secure in our beliefs, more open-minded to those who share our current and past beliefs, and all-around better individuals. We have many chances throughout our day to use our intellectual courage, and soon enough, it won't feel nearly as hard as it was before.

Intellectual empathy

We all watch those cheesy movies that have a mean boss who never lets any of the employees off the hook. You'll see people come up and say things like "My child is sick, I need to pick them up." or "My grandfather passed away, and I need time off for the funeral." It never fails; the mean boss always denies whatever their request is. We are sitting on the sidelines (our couch) and silently cursing all the mean bosses of the world as we scream, "Do you have no empathy?"

And so we are here. Intellectual empathy. What does it mean? How can you practice it?

Intellectual empathy means that you have the conscious knowledge that you need to put yourself in the other person's shoes so that you can understand them. This is actually a lot harder than it might seem while you are reading about it. And this trait doesn't just kick in when something serious like a death happens. No, this is a trait that you should be using every day when someone else presents their point of view on a topic.

If we scoff and laugh anytime someone opens their mouth and raises a point that is different from our own, our intellectual empathy is not among our top three strengths. To create a respectful and empathetic environment where everyone can feel comfortable enough to share their viewpoints, we need to imagine what that person is thinking, feeling, and where they are coming from.

A person who was raised in a low-income household is going to have a much different view on government support than a person who was raised in a mansion by the sea. These two people have every opportunity to laugh at the other person's view, but if they are practicing intellectual empathy, they will try to understand. The rich person will try to think about what it must have been like to know that without the government support their colleague received, they never would have survived. And the low-income household person needs to try and understand where the rich person is coming from, and where they may have seen the system abused in cities near them.

The two people need to reason from the other's point of view. This would be practicing intellectual empathy.

However, that's not where this trait stops. Don't we all love to admit when we are wrong? I know that I absolutely hate it. I wish I could say that I love it, but I don't.

Practicing intellectual empathy means that you have to remember when you were wrong in the past. Even when you think you are 100% right and there is no way that you are wrong, remember that you've been wrong in the past. Once you remember that, try to apply it to the situation at hand. Is there a chance you are wrong now? If you honestly still believe you are right, remember that the other person also believes that they are right. The least you can do is treat them fairly, because no one likes to be wrong. Empathize with the person whether they are right or wrong.

Intellectual autonomy

Let's talk about autonomy for a minute and why it is so hard for us humans to practice. You know all those cute little animal videos you watch on the internet? The ones that always get me are the giraffes and deer. Something about their tiny, unbalanced legs just pulls me into watching the screen. They are seriously adorable, and I cannot get enough. It always amazes me that after a few moments, these animals can walk. From the time they are babies, they are doing things for themselves. Some animals don't even stay with their parents. How crazy is that?

Humans, on the other hand, are helpless. So helpless. And not just for a few days, but for years and years and years! Even when a child can walk and talk, they still need care. It isn't until they are 16-20 years old that they can live by themselves, pay their taxes, secure a job, and be a normal and rational human being.

Autonomy is basically thinking and doing things for yourself, and humans just aren't the best at it, probably because we live with our parents for so long. My mother would always tell me that it was illegal to have the inside car light on when we were driving at night. Because I was a child, I blindly believed her. I believed her for so long that it is honestly embarrassing. I won't admit at what age I found out that it is not illegal to have the inside car light on when it is dark. Seriously, it hurts the ego too much. But I believed her because she was my mother, so she had to be telling the truth.

If you haven't figured it out by now, our parents aren't always right. Sure, they did their best, and most of them do a great job. But their views and their thoughts are completely their own, and we don't have to blindly accept and believe them.

Intellectual autonomy deals with having rational control over what you believe, value, and infer. You have to learn to think for yourself and know how to handle your thought processes. Analyze and evaluate situations on hand and then learn when you should believe, conform, or question. If your mom told you at 30 years old that it's illegal to keep the light in your car on, you'd probably just laugh. That seems so silly. You have to learn how to choose what to believe and what to question. If something feels off to you, it probably is.

Let's say your boss says, "No, it's okay to just sign the person up even though they said not to. That's how we do our business." Does that seem fishy to you? Should you be questioning it? Your boss is telling you what to think and do, but someone practicing intellectual autonomy will have a siren going off in their brain saying

"Question this!" Commit to use autonomy to think for yourself.

Intellectual integrity

We'd like to think we practice integrity because it is important. Let me tell you a story of my old friend Jane. She was the messiest person ever. I always wanted her to clean up after herself and her dishes, but she never seemed to do it. This got frustrating after a while, so I confronted her about it. I asked Jane why she never did her dishes and she made me do them for her. Jane was completely confused. Her response was, "I thought this whole time that you were doing the dishes and I was doing the laundry."

So I had to stop and think, had I done any laundry lately? I don't know if I thought a magic genie was doing my laundry or not, but I was so focused on the lack of Jane doing her dishes that I didn't realize that I hadn't been doing *any* laundry. It turned out that I wasn't holding myself to the same standards I was holding Jane to. And guess what? This happens all the time.

How often do you get mad at your roommate or spouse for not doing something? Maybe your friend keeps doing the same thing over and over again and it drives you crazy. Take a step back and think about what you're doing, or what you are *not* doing. Too often, we hold people to unrealistic expectations. Think of it like this: When we view ourselves, we place this golden halo over our head and think that we are doing everything perfectly. When we think of people who are frustrating us, we place devil horns on the sides of their head. But we don't realize how unfair this is. Shatter the halo and devil horns and put yourself on one side and your friend on the other side of a scale. This scale should be balanced.

Practicing intellectual integrity means that we are holding others to the same standards that we hold ourselves to. We need to be consistent about this and hold ourselves to the high standard that we inevitably hold everyone else to.

It's okay to hold rigorous standards for everyone else, but you better make sure that you're hitting those standards as well. Whenever you're in an argument with someone else, make sure that you are acting with integrity.

Be true to what you are thinking and what you are putting out on the table. If you're preaching recycling, don't throw a paper cup into the garbage and expect to be acting with integrity. Do what you say you are going to do and practice what you preach. You think recycling is important? Then you better make sure you are recycling every bottle and can at your house before you preach to someone else about their failure to do so.

Intellectual perseverance

Perseverance is hard. If you played a game as a child and saw that you were about to lose, what did you do? A lot of younger kids will suddenly start saying that the game is unfair, that it's rigged, and that they need to start over. We *love* to give up when things are hard. However, when we do give up, we don't learn anything.

There are many situations in life where you're going to feel like giving up, stopping, or starting over. This happens in our personal lives, our educational lives, and our business lives.

Intellectual perseverance means that you realize you need to use insights, even when things get too hard or difficult. When you are frustrated and there are way too many obstacles in front of you, you should adhere firmly to the rational principles that you know. Even if there is opposition from everyone around you, even if you need to be confused and struggle over lots of questions, even if it takes a really long time, you have to persevere. Because when you do persevere, you achieve a much deeper understanding or insight.

Intellectual perseverance is the action of persisting when life gets tough. This trait will help you out in the long run in your professional and personal life.

Confidence in reason

Confidence in reason happens by encouraging people to make up their own minds, encouraging others to draw their own conclusions and develop their own rational beliefs and values. It also means that you rely on faith and know that in the end, people can be rational, see from others' viewpoints, think for themselves, think critically and logically concerning arguments and presented situations, and draw meaningful and reasonable conclusions. It is the hope that we will all become reasonable people and persuade each other with rationality, rather than anything else.

However, there are a lot of things in society and in our minds that are against us on this. For one, lots of people like control. Control is a hard thing to give up, and every time someone has a different viewpoint than we do, we try to convince them to adopt ours. It is an innate desire to control the situation at hand. Call it some caveman alpha thing or just the regular human brain, but we have a problem remembering that if someone has a different viewpoint, it isn't automatically wrong.

When you have confidence in reason, you are secure in the fact that your viewpoint is right to you because of the reasoning you present to your own beliefs, but you're also confident that the person in front of you has their belief that is right to them because of the reasons that align with *their* beliefs. This can be a bit confusing, so I'm going to strip it down to an easy example to understand.

Let's say there are two people named Joe and Marty. They both want candy, but there are two candy shops that are right next door to each other. Joe wants to go to the candy shop on the right, but Marty wants to go to the candy shop on the left. Joe says that the candy shop on the right is the better way to go because they have endless sour gummy worms. Marty says that the candy shop on the left is the way to go because they import the finest chocolates.

Well, which candy store is right and which one is wrong? They both have reasons for why each candy shop is better, and their reasoning is correct. Joe loves gummy worms and Marty loves chocolate. So for Joe, the candy store on the right is the correct choice because they have endless gummy worms. And for Marty, the candy store on the left is the correct choice because they have the best chocolate.

When they realize that they both want different things, Joe and Marty decide to go to the separate candy shops and then meet back outside. They are confident that they are each making the right choice.

Just because someone else has a different view doesn't mean they are wrong. Sometimes, you'll be able to convince them that the way you view things with your reasoning is correct, and other times, there is no right or wrong. You should have confidence in your reasoning and know that in the end, it will all work out.

Fair-mindedness

I talked earlier how we always like to think that life isn't fair. Situations aren't always fair, but we can still practice at being fair-minded. We can refrain biasing ourselves in favor of someone just because they might share our point of view.

If you are practicing this trait, you are treating all viewpoints with the same tenacity. This means that you are not giving preference to someone you know loves to do the same thing as you.

This becomes a big concern with people who are making decisions. Take, for example, a person who is interviewing job prospects. They see that one of them graduated from NYU, and the interviewer *also* graduated from NYU. Even though the other resume in front of them is more qualified for the job, they end up calling the person who attended NYU because they felt an immediate bias toward them.

This can also work against people, like when someone is a woman or a different race. Maybe the woman is much more qualified for the job, but the employer suddenly thinks, "Well, I don't want to hire someone who is just going to leave in a year to have children."

Can you think of a time that you were treated unfairly? There have been times that you have been rejected, but I mean a time that you were rejected or treated differently because of your views or beliefs? Maybe it was a cashier at the store, perhaps it was your boss, or maybe it was even a friend or family member. How did it feel?

I know that when I've been treated unfairly, it hurts. It feels like you are completely helpless and that you couldn't have done anything to make the situation better. If we know how much it sucks, why do we do it to others? You don't need to put someone down because their views are different than yours. Even if you are on two ends of a spectrum, they deserve the respect of being treated fairly.

If we are practicing being fair-minded, we know that it is extremely important to treat everyone the same. No matter what our own feelings or interests are, or the feelings of our friends or community, we need to adhere to our intellectual standards and not bring in our own thoughts and feelings toward others.

Chapter 5: Quick Tips

There are a few steps you can take to help develop your critical thinking skills.

1. Question those assumptions.

We make assumptions all day, every day. We see a homeless person on the street and immediately think they are a drug addict. When our friend doesn't text us, we think they must be mad at us. Our brain is trying to process little pieces of information, and it is how we end up getting by each day. Assumptions are the foundation of how we think, but they aren't always right. In fact, a lot of times, they are wrong.

When you question your assumptions, you can try to describe what happened and start from scratch. Lots of our assumptions will fail. You can ask, for example, "Why do I think that my friend is mad at me just because I haven't heard from them today?"

2. Accepting information.

Let's say someone comes up to you and says that the sky is blue because it is a reflection of the ocean. To those in California, that might seem true. To those in Nebraska, that seems pretty false. You shouldn't just blindly accept information that you haven't investigated yourself. Instead of analyzing everything that comes our way, we usually either accept or deny information based on who it is coming from. We more readily accept information from trustworthy people, whereas when it comes to untrustworthy people's testimony, we are quicker to deny.

However, that leaves a lot unsettled. Instead of going by trustworthy and untrustworthy, try going by your gut instinct. You either think something is right or you think it sounds fishy. When your gut tells you it is questionable, go and look up the information yourself.

3. Question things.

It might seem a bit redundant, but asking questions is one of the most important parts of critical thinking. Ask yourself questions all the time about anything that pops into your mind. The more questions you ask, the better you'll get at asking them and acquiring answers.

4. Understand biases.

We are pretty judgmental creatures, so we need to understand that we have a lot of biases in our lives. You should try to understand what your biases are.

5. Think ahead.

We should all be thinking ahead, but I mean *really* think ahead. You shouldn't just think about what you are doing tomorrow; you should be thinking about what you are doing the next several weeks, months, and years. Thinking ahead can help you outwit every problem that comes your way. Just imagine that you are playing a game where you are trying to predict your opponent's next move.

Jeff Bezos, the CEO of Amazon, said this about thinking ahead: "If everything you do needs to work on a three-year time horizon, then you're competing against a lot of people. But if you're willing to invest on a seven-year time horizon, you're now competing against a fraction of those people, because very few companies are willing to do that."[xviii]

6. Read.

Your mind needs a workout, and it needs to be a restorative and relaxing workout. Would you imagine that you can get that by reading? Reading a good book has the power to open up your mind, release your emotions, or enlighten you on different subjects. Elon Musk is a big proponent of reading, and he says that it helped him master rocket science. So, hey, anything is possible.

7. Be empathetic.

You should have no problem putting yourself in others' shoes. It is important to see where people are coming from, and it's a great way to help you develop your critical thinking skills. Imagine others' motivations, problems, and dreams.

8. Have options.

Try to understand that you have options, and that there's never only one route to go. Weigh them and try to think of the different options that might be out there that you aren't thinking of.

9. Surround yourself with people smarter than you are.

We all love being a big fish in a small pond, but being a little fish in a big pond might actually be better. To get better at something, you need to be surrounded by people who are better than you. You become like the five people you hang out around the most, so make sure you're hanging out with some smart people. You can learn a lot from them.

10. Don't be absolute.

We love to use "never" and "always" in arguments, but they are hardly ever true. Absolutes should be avoided at all costs. However, you should also be assertive. Don't think that throwing out absolutes makes it so you can't tell people how things are, if you need to.

11. Be diplomatic.

Ask for others' opinions on a certain proposal. You are not rejecting a person, just a proposal. Asking for other opinions could help change your approach. The more opinions, the better. There are always people with better understanding of a certain age group or community than you.

12. Critique and practice.

Practice critiquing others in a kind way. There is a tactful way to do this, so read up on other critiques until you learn how to develop your own style.

How Could You Ask Questions in Different Situations?[xix]

Remembering: The purpose of this is to memorize or recall something, so your questions should be about identifying, retrieving, naming, or recognizing. Try something along the lines of "What do we already know about recycling?" or "How does recycling tie in with what we learned about oceans?"

Understanding: The purpose of this is to find the meaning of something you have heard. The questions should be able to describe or explain further. Try "What will happen if we enact recycling programs?" or "Explain how recycling will help the ocean."

Applying: The purpose of this is to apply your knowledge, so your questions should implement or solve what you've heard. Try "How could recycling help save animals?" or "What is the obstacle against recycling?"

Analyzing: The goal of this is to break down the information presented to you. Questions can help compare or organize the information. Try asking "Why is recycling important?" or "What is the difference between recycling and composting?"

Evaluating: This is used to judge or decide what to do when information is presented. The questions need to check, critique, and explain. Try "How does recycling affect animals?" or "What is the best way to recycle, and why?"

Creating: The goal here is to combine everything to form a new solution or pattern. The questions asked need to design or construct. Try asking "What is the solution to the problem of people not knowing what to recycle?" or "What is another way to look at recycling plastic?"

Chapter 6: Barriers to Critical Thinking

We all make assumptions and decisions based on influence from others, as well as our own personal interests, but that can all disappear if we learn to think critically. In this chapter, I'll go over how you can think critically and do away with the limitations holding you back so you never find yourself in another situation where you judged too soon or unfairly.

Egocentrism[xx]

We spend a lot of time thinking about our own wants, desires, and needs. There are certain times in our lives when we think even more about ourselves, like when we go through a tough breakup.

When we think about everything with self-interested thinking, we cannot think objectively. We let our own needs get in the way when we are making a decision, and that can be detrimental to others. We tend to think of ourselves as being more important than other people, and that is considered to be egocentrism.

While it may sound similar, this is not the same as narcissism. Egocentric people do not feel better when they admire themselves, they just think that they are the center of attention. It appears more frequently in childhood, but it can still exist in adults. Research has found that when we make quick judgments, we are very egocentric. It is a natural process for us to not consider the needs of others. We believe that our intuitions are correct, even if they are far from it.[xxi]

Sociocentrism

This occurs when we think our social group is superior to that of others. We end up thinking that the people like us are much less at fault than those who are unlike us. This social pressure makes us sacrifice our own critical thinking. Just think of the tunnel vision you are experiencing!

While you are focusing on more than yourself, you're still only focusing on those who are like you. While it is different than egocentrism, it still creates the same bias toward others.

Inconsistencies[xxii]

Inconsistency fallacy is the logic hiccup where two or more propositions are asserted but cannot both possibly be true. In everyday life, it would translate to holding two or more beliefs that cannot all be true at the same time.

The inconsistency fallacy is something critical thinkers try to avoid because their arguments and opinions should be consistent. Here is a classic statement: "I'm all for equal rights for women. I just think a woman's place is in the home." It just doesn't make sense.

There is also practical inconsistency where you might say you believe one thing, but then do the other. For example, "I'm a strong believer in freedom of speech and think artists should never be censored. However, when musicians like Marilyn Manson influence the youth, you have to draw a line and say no more."[xxiii]

Prejudice

We could say, "Prejudice is the antithesis of critical thinking. Prejudice literally means to pre-judge—that is, to render judgment prior to having relevant information. A critical thinker tends, where possible, to wait for the relevant information, before rendering judgment.

When you are prejudiced (against a certain group of people, for example) you are emotionally primed to jump to conclusions whenever you meet an individual from that group."[xxiv]

Fear

Fear can prevent you from asking the right questions or going against evidence that doesn't seem right. This can happen at both an individual and institutional level.

Laziness

Critical thinking is going to take some effort on your part, so laziness cannot work with it. If you are not willing to explore, critical thinking doesn't work.

Pride

It squashes the ability to admit that you are wrong. You need to also embrace when you are wrong to be able to be closer to the "truth."

Peer pressure

As I was researching the relationship between peer pressure and critical thinking, I found a great analysis of it by Bruce R. Bain.

"Peer relationships are usually based upon the unstated premise that most members of the peer group will agree with each other on all subjects, and also that nobody will challenge any presumption in the thought or mindset of the group. Peer groups, gangs, or even just social cliques often demonstrate a kind of mutual bonding based upon strong feelings of insecurity.

If 'creativity' or individuality shows at all in such groups, it is usually shown by outward appearance. Dyed hair, a certain way of dressing, tattoos, and the use of certain idiomatic expressions in spoken communications that are unique to the particular peer group are common, or merely the assumption that any 'creativity,' if shown at all, should be 'weird' and unconventional.

Sometimes, the members of such a group choose to 'appear' to be a threat to anyone else. This is intended to bestow upon all members of the peer group a sense of power over those not in the peer group. Anti-social attitudes, or general messages which suggest 'I—Don't—Care,' are common to such groups.

Such peer groups may have either a high or a low social status. They may show either wealth or poverty, very educated or poorly educated, athletic or even physically degenerate and dissolute. (...)

Examination of the processes associated with critical thinking shows something quite the opposite. Critical thinking is not specific, intended to show agreement to any proposition without thought, without an examination of facts, and without any examination of the reasoning that serves for the basis of any proposition.

Critical thinking is designed to objectively challenge all assumptions and to challenge all conclusions in an objective way. If anything, critical thinking serves to exclude a person, in specific, from 'social acceptance.'

The only peer group where a critical thinker will find acceptance generally, would be amongst other persons in the knowledge disciplines such as science, mathematics, law, philosophy, theology, and historiography, and possibly some peer groups in the fine arts such as literature, etc.

So there can be peer groups in which critical thinking is a necessary precondition.

But those mentioned have, for their purpose, a knowledge that is quite distinct from mere 'social acceptance.' It is not a 'unique' individual self that is published or shown for consideration. It is knowledge itself that is shown for public acceptance or rejection. (…)"[xxv]

Wishful thinking

Wishful thinking is when we desire for something to be true but we use this wish as evidence for the truthfulness of the claim. This cognitive bias can also turn someone's evaluation of the evidence differently based on the desired outcome. For example, when you are in a terrible relationship, but you stick to your guns that things will change if only this or that happens. "I know in my heart of hearts that they will be more loving with me in the future."

No, you don't know that. The best predictor for the future is largely the past, unless some dramatic change occurs in the present that would indicate otherwise. And what the heck is your "heart of hearts" anyway?

Hate

A strong emotion like hate will influence your point of view about anything, really. If you hate something, or someone, there is no chance in a million years you'll be objective about it without very strong deliberation and discipline. Even then, you might tilt reality based on your emotions. Be careful when you want to create a critical thinking agenda around such a topic. It is often better to just leave the decision-making to someone who is not so emotionally involved in the question. Or wait until you feel somewhat better about the topic.

Sometimes we are self-centered in our standards, and this is what causes us to believe or reject something. Here are some common things that happen when we think:

- "It's true because I believe it.— Egocentrism.
- It's true because we believe it.— Sociocentrism.
- It's true because I want to believe it.— Wish fulfillment, believing whatever puts you in a positive light and feels good.
- It's true because I have always believed it.—Self-validation, wanting to maintain beliefs that you have believed for a long time.
- It's true because it is in my best interest to believe it.—Selfishness, believing

whatever gets you more power, wealth, or advantage."[xxvi]

Now ask yourself some of these questions:

- What is my goal with practicing critical thinking skills?
- What are the pros and cons of critical thinking?
- Why is this skill important to me?
- How can I overcome the barriers of critical thinking?
- How can I communicate with others who don't think critically?
- How can I respond when there's a lack of critical thinking?

Chapter 7: Critical Thinking Exercises

Type 1 Exercises:

Read a non-fiction book

Reading non-fiction can help challenge the way you think about certain things. It opens up topics for debate, and it helps provoke some thoughts you may not have considered otherwise. Read a book and focus on the emotions the book elicits from you. Why? Do you agree with the author? Why? Do you disagree and the book makes you tense? Even better. Why? What would you prefer the author was saying? Why?

Find a problem to solve

Small problems are still problems. Find a small problem in your life or in the world and try to solve it. Devote your time to this problem and come up with reasonable solutions. How would you start solving this problem? What would it take? What unintended consequences could follow this solution? For example, you want to help Stan, the homeless guy from the corner. How would you solve Stan's problem? Could this solution be extended to the problem of homelessness overall? Why? Why not?

Talk to someone you consider smarter than you are

I'm sure there are many people who would love to go out to lunch and talk to you about some of their ideas. There are always problems and questions that keep people awake at night. Listening to these people can help you broaden your perspective on ideas, problems, and solutions.

Practice teamwork

The older we get, the less we work with teams. However, working with a team can provide a valuable learning curve on things you were stuck for ages with on your own. Get together with some of your coworkers and work on something, join a mastermind group in your local community, join a club of any kind. Share information and time with likeminded and totally different people.

Write in a journal

Many of us stop journaling when we get out of school, but it is actually really important to keep doing it. A journal can help you jot down emotions, experiences, and ideas that you might forget otherwise. Things that can be great to check in the years to come. Journaling is also a form of meditation and self-made therapy.

Type 2 Exercises:

Tour guide for a foreigner

Imagine that you're giving a tour in your town for someone who comes from a different continent. For lunch you take your tourist to an all-you-can-eat buffet. He has never gone to an all-you-can-eat buffet before so he is very confused. Answer the following questions as if the foreigner would ask them:

- What is a buffet?
- Why is there endless food?
- Why do people like stuffing themselves full?

- Why don't you always eat at buffets?

We assume that everyone knows what a buffet is, but that's something we take for granted. You are being forced to look deeper at some of the things that seem normal to us.

Fact of opinion

It isn't always easy to tell what is fact and what's opinion. You need trustworthy sources to tell you facts. Get with a friend or partner and try to figure out if each statement is a fact or opinion:

- My boss is the best boss ever.
- My iPhone is hard to operate.
- The deepest part of the ocean is over 35,000 feet deep.
- Doing drugs is bad for your health.
- Going out to eat is fun.

- Your boss is boring.

- One in 100 people are colorblind.

- Thin Mint cookies are the best Girl Scout cookie.

- Doing work is hard.

Some of these might be easier to judge than others. If you and your partner come up with different answers, it is most likely an opinion and not a fact.

Type 3 Exercise: The Warren Buffet Special

Warren Buffet's critical thinking exercise is quite interesting. He used to jot down ten companies that were the highest performers in each given year. He would keep a record of the names of the companies, and then he kept track of what happened to those companies 10-20 years later. Sometimes they did well, sometimes they failed miserably. He liked to see what led to their rise or fall and how they had fared over the years.

This exercise is really helpful towards critical thinking. You don't have to find the top-performing companies, but you could follow trends of what you are interested in. Look to see what survived in fashion over 20 years, read about the changes in nutrition, or look at the evolvement of bodybuilding from when it started to now. Anything you are interested in can be looked at the same way Warren Buffet looked at businesses.[xxvii]

Type 4 Exercise:

For these exercises, try to defend your stance with logic, reasoning, knowledge, and common sense. Go through it four times and try out your answers with each of those traits.

1. You witness a coworker sharing confidential files, but you read that the email is to the local authorities and your company is committing fraud. Do you report the coworker to the boss for breaching security, or leave the situation alone since it was sent to the government?

2. You find a $100 bill on the ground but didn't see anyone around you drop it. Do you keep it for yourself, ask the other people in line at the store, or donate the money?

3. A police officer pulls over someone for speeding. However, it is his niece in the car. Should he: give her the ticket since

she broke the law, or let her go and pretend it never happened?

Final Thoughts

Question what you hear. Question what you read. Think about the author's biases and the motivations behind their opinion. People can be emotionally influenced when they say something—they might overlook something or interpret the data they talk about incorrectly. You can't know for sure unless you take the time to gather confirmatory evidence.

Ask yourself "How could it be wrong?" every time you read or hear something you instantly agree with. Track how long it takes you to come up with an alternative opinion—contradictory with what you reflexively agreed with before.

There are other important aspects to analyze in our consumerist 21st century. For example, ask yourself how the author of an article could benefit from saying or writing something. Or see if the information you read about triggers something relevant or relatable in your life, and that's why you agree or disagree. Sometimes your emotional memory validates certain information that logically would be neutral or untrue.

One thing is for sure, there is very little on this Earth we can know with absolute certainty. Even studies and research can have distorted or biased empirical support behind them. For instance, many studies use subjects from similar environments (a school, a neighborhood) or with similar aptitude (people who are willing to participate in the study), which makes the study's broader relevance questionable.

Everything should be taken with a grain of salt—even what I'm telling you right now. Everything in this world can be questioned. At the end of the day, the better we can navigate between uncertainties and big questions, the deeper understanding we will gain of the world we live in. In my opinion, this is a far greater skill to have than to be able to memorize some numbers and names in history class. But this is my opinion. Please, question it.

I believe in you!

Yours truly,

Zoe

Reference

Ambler, George. *Learn to Think Long-Term Like Jeff Bezos*. George Ambler. 2014. http://www.georgeambler.com/learn-think-long-term-like-jeff-bezos/

Austin, Michael W. Ph.D. *Standards of Critical Thinking*. Psychology Today. 2012. https://www.psychologytoday.com/blog/ethics-everyone/201206/standards-critical-thinking

Assessment, Insight. *Characteristics of Strong Critical Thinkers*. Insights Assessment. 2017. https://www.insightassessment.com/Resources/Importance-of-Critical-Thinking/Characteristics-of-Strong-Critical-Thinkers

Assessment, Insight. *Expert Consensus on Critical Thinking*. Insight Assessment. 2017. https://www.insightassessment.com/Resources/Importance-of-Critical-Thinking/Expert-Consensus-on-Critical-Thinking

Assessment, Insight. *Expert Consensus on Critical Thinking*. Insight Assessment. 2017.

https://www.insightassessment.com/Resources/I
mportance-of-Critical-Thinking/Expert-Consensus-
on-Critical-Thinking

Baer, Drake. *Here's How To Do Warren Buffett's Favorite Critical Thinking Exercise*. Business Insider. 2014.
http://www.businessinsider.com/warren-
buffetts-favorite-critical-thinking-exercise-2014-
10

Brown University. *Questions Provoking Critical Thinking*. Based on: "Alison King, "Inquiring Minds Really Do Want to Know: Using Questioning to Teach Critical Thinking," Teaching of Psychology 22 (1995): 14." Brown University. 2017.
https://www.brown.edu/about/administration/s
heridan-center/teaching-learning/effective-
classroom-practices/discussions-
seminars/questions

Cherry, Kendra. *Concrete Operational Stage of Cognitive Development*. Very Well. 2017.
https://www.verywell.com/concrete-operational-
stage-of-cognitive-development-2795458

Cherry, Kendra. *Formal Operational Stage of Cognitive Development*. 2017.
https://www.verywell.com/formal-operational-
stage-of-cognitive-development-2795459

Cherry, Kendra. *Preoperational Stage of Cognitive Development*. Very Well. 2017.
https://www.verywell.com/preoperational-stage-of-cognitive-development-2795461

Cherry, Kendra. *What Happens During the Sensorimotor Stage of Cognitive Development*? Very Well. 2017.
https://www.verywell.com/sensorimotor-stage-of-cognitive-development-2795462

DeLecce, Tara. *What is Critical Thinking? - Definition, Skills & Meaning*. Study. 2017.
http://study.com/academy/lesson/what-is-critical-thinking-definition-skills-meaning.html

Elder, Linda. Paul, Richard. *The Analysis & Assessment of Thinking*. The Foundation for Critical Thinking. 2008.
http://www.criticalthinking.org/pages/the-analysis-amp-assessment-of-thinking/497

Elder, Linda. Paul, Richard. *Universal Intellectual Standards*. The Foundation for Critical Thinking. 2010.
http://www.criticalthinking.org/pages/universal-intellectual-standards/527

Gilkey, Roderick. Caceda, Ricardo. Kilts, Clinton. *When Emotional Reasoning Trumps IQ.* Harvard Business Review. 2010. https://hbr.org/2010/09/when-emotional-reasoning-trumps-iq

O'Reilley, Kim. Ph.D. *Why Critical Thinking Is So Important.* Intercultural Solutions. 2008. https://www.interculturalsolutions.net/why-critical-thinking-is-so-important/

Russel, Robert. *What Are Four Barriers to Critical Thinking?* Classroom. 2017. http://classroom.synonym.com/four-barriers-critical-thinking-8427849.html

S. Abbott (Ed.), *The glossary of education reform.* Retrieved from http://edglossary.org/hidden-curriculum. 2014. http://edglossary.org/critical-thinking/

Scientific American. *Do we really use only 10 percent of our brains?* Scientific American. 2017. https://www.scientificamerican.com/article/do-we-really-use-only-10/

Serva, Christine. *Common Barriers to Critical Thinking.* Study. 2017. http://study.com/academy/lesson/common-barriers-to-critical-thinking.html

The Foundation for Critical Thinking. *Critical Thinking: Where to Begin*. The Foundation for Critical Thinking. 2017. http://www.criticalthinking.org/pages/critical-thinking-where-to-begin/796

The Foundation For Critical Thinking. *Valuable Intellectual Traits.* The Foundation for Critical Thinking. 2017. http://www.criticalthinking.org/pages/valuable-intellectual-traits/528

University of Louisville. *Paul-Elder Critical Thinking Framework.* Based on: "Paul, R. and Elder, L. (2010). The Miniature Guide to Critical Thinking Concepts and Tools. Dillon Beach: Foundation for Critical Thinking Press." University of Louisville. 2017. http://louisville.edu/ideastoaction/about/criticalthinking/framework

Wade, Carole. Tavris, Carol. *Psychology*. 5th edition. Longman Publishers. 1998.

Still With Me?

How did you like The Critical Mind? Would you consider leaving a feedback about your reading experience so other readers could know about it? If you are willing to sacrifice some of your time to do so, there are several options you can do it:

1. Leave a review on Amazon
   https://www.amazon.com/dp/B07ZS2VDWK
2. Leave a review on goodreads.com. Here is a link to my profile where you find all of my books.
   https://www.goodreads.com/author/show/14967542.Zoe_McKey
3. Send me a private message to
   zoemckey@gmail.com
4. Tell your friends and family about your reading experience.

Your feedback is very valuable to me to assess if I'm on the good path providing help to you and where do I need to improve. Your feedback is also valuable to other people as they can learn about my work and perhaps give an independent author as myself a chance. I deeply appreciate any kind of feedback you take time to provide me.

Thank you so much for choosing to read my book among the many out there. If you'd like to receive an update once I have a new book, you can subscribe to my newsletter at www.zoemckey.com. You'll get My Daily Routine Makeover cheat sheet and Unbreakable Confidence checklist for FREE. You'll also get occasional book recommendations from other authors I trust and know they deliver good quality books.

Brave Enough

Time to learn how to overcome the feeling of inferiority and achieve success. Brave Enough takes you step by step through the process of understanding the nature of your fears, overcome limiting beliefs and gain confidence with the help of studies, personal stories and actionable exercises at the end of each chapter.

Say goodbye to fear of rejection and inferiority complex once and for all.

Less Mess Less Stress

Don't compromise with your happiness. "Good enough" is not the life you deserve - you deserve the best, and the good news is that you can have it. Learn the surprising truth that it's not by doing more, but less with Less Mess Less Stress.

We know that we own too much, we say yes for too many engagements, and we stick to more than we should. Physical, mental and relationship clutter are daily burdens we have to deal with. Change your mindset and live a happier life with less.

Minimalist Budget

Minimalist Budget will help you to turn your bloated expenses into a well-toned budget, spending on exactly what you need and nothing else.

This book presents solutions for two major problems in our consumer society: (1) how to downsize your cravings without having to sacrifice the fun stuff, and (2) how to whip your finances into shape and follow a personalized budget.

Rewire Your Habits

Rewire Your Habits discusses which habits one should adopt to make changes in 5 life areas: self-improvement, relationships, money management, health, and free time. The book addresses every goal-setting, habit building challenge in these areas and breaks them down with simplicity and ease.

Tame Your Emotions

Tame Your Emotions is a collection of the most common and painful emotional insecurities and their antidotes. Even the most successful people have fears and self-sabotaging habits. But they also know how to use them to their advantage and keep their fears on a short leash. This is exactly what my book will teach you – using the tactics of experts and research-proven methods.

Emotions can't be eradicated. But they can be controlled.

The Art of Minimalism

The Art of Minimalism will present you 4 minimalist techniques, the bests from around the world, to give you a perspective on how to declutter your house, your mind, and your life in general. Learn how to let go of everything that is not important in your life and find methods that give you a peace of mind and happiness instead.

Keep balance at the edge of minimalism and consumerism.

The Disciplined Mind

Where you end up in life is determined by a number of times you fall and get up, and how much pain and discomfort you can withstand along the way. The path to an extraordinary accomplishment and a life worth living is not innate talent, but focus, willpower, and disciplined action.

Maximize your brain power and keep in control of your thoughts.

In The Disciplined Mind, you will find unique lessons through which you will learn those essential steps and qualities that are needed to reach your goals easier and faster.

The Mind-Changing Habit of Journaling

Understand where your negative self-image, bad habits, and unhealthy thoughts come from. Know yourself to change yourself. Embrace the life-changing transformation potential of journaling. This book shows you how to use the ultimate self-healing tool of journaling to find your own answers to your most pressing problems, discover your true self and lead a life of growth mindset.

The Unlimited Mind

This book collects all the tips, tricks and tactics of the most successful people to develop your inner smartness.

The Unlimited Mind will show you how to think smarter and find your inner genius. This book is a collection of research and scientific studies about better decision-making, fairer judgments, and intuition improvement. It takes a critical look at our everyday cognitive habits and points out small but serious mistakes that are easily correctable.

Who You Were Meant To Be

Discover the strengths of your personality and how to use them to make better life choices. In Who You Were Born To Be, you'll learn some of the most influential personality-related studies. Thanks to these studies you'll learn to capitalize on your strengths, and how you can you become the best version of yourself.

Wired For Confidence

Do you feel like you just aren't good enough? End this vicious thought cycle NOW. Wired For Confidence tells you the necessary steps to break out from the pits of low self-esteem, lowered expectations, and lack of assertiveness. Take the first step to creating the life you only dared to dream of.

To access the full list of my books visit this link.

Endnotes

[i] Scientific American. *Do we really use only 10 percent of our brains?* Scientific American. 2017. https://www.scientificamerican.com/article/do-we-really-use-only-10/

[ii] Media. A tenyekben volt a legtobb krimi. Media. 2017. https://media1.hu/2019/06/07/a-tenyekben-volt-a-legtobb-krimi-az-m1-hirado-musoridejenek-37-szazaleka-migracios-buncselekmenyekrol-szolt/

[iii] Biro, Marianna. Szemann Tamas. Migracios Valsag. Index. 2019. https://index.hu/belfold/2019/03/06/migracios_valsag_tomeges_bevandorlas_miatti_valsaghelyzet_magyarorszagon/?token=35c961db5df5820e3e94b360e40dfff2

[iv] DeLecce, Tara. *What is Critical Thinking? - Definition, Skills & Meaning.* Study. 2017. http://study.com/academy/lesson/what-is-critical-thinking-definition-skills-meaning.html

[v] Wade, Carole. Tavris, Carol. *Psychology.* 5th edition. Longman Publishers. 1998.

[vi] Assessment, Insight. *Characteristics of Strong Critical Thinkers.* Insights Assessment. 2017.

https://www.insightassessment.com/Resources/Importance-of-Critical-Thinking/Characteristics-of-Strong-Critical-Thinkers

[vii] Cherry, Kendra. *What Happens During the Sensorimotor Stage of Cognitive Development?* Very Well. 2017. https://www.verywell.com/sensorimotor-stage-of-cognitive-development-2795462

[viii] Cherry, Kendra. *Preoperational Stage of Cognitive Development.* Very Well. 2017. https://www.verywell.com/preoperational-stage-of-cognitive-development-2795461

[ix] Cherry, Kendra. *Concrete Operational Stage of Cognitive Development.* Very Well. 2017. https://www.verywell.com/concrete-operational-stage-of-cognitive-development-2795458

[x] Cherry, Kendra. *Formal Operational Stage of Cognitive Development.* 2017. https://www.verywell.com/formal-operational-stage-of-cognitive-development-2795459

[xi] Creative and Critical Thinking. Critical Thinking and the Three Stages of Cognitive Development. Creative and Critical Thinking. 2019. https://creativityandcriticalthinking.wordpress.com/the-evolution-from-pre-k-to-college/critical-thinking-and-the-three-stages-of-cognitive-development/

[xii] Harvard Health Publishing. Can vitamin C prevent a cold? Harvard Health Publishing. 2017.

https://www.health.harvard.edu/cold-and-flu/can-vitamin-c-prevent-a-cold

[xiii] Gilkey, Roderick. Caceda, Ricardo. Kilts, Clinton. *When Emotional Reasoning Trumps IQ.* Harvard Business Review. 2010. https://hbr.org/2010/09/when-emotional-reasoning-trumps-iq

[xiv] Elder, Linda. Paul, Richard. *Universal Intellectual Standards.* The Foundation for Critical Thinking. 2010. http://www.criticalthinking.org/pages/universal-intellectual-standards/527

[xv] Elder, Linda. Paul, Richard. *The Analysis & Assessment of Thinking.* The Foundation for Critical Thinking. 2008. http://www.criticalthinking.org/pages/the-analysis-amp-assessment-of-thinking/497

[xvi] University of Louisville. *Paul-Elder Critical Thinking Framework.* Based on: "Paul, R. and Elder, L. (2010). The Miniature Guide to Critical Thinking Concepts and Tools. Dillon Beach: Foundation for Critical Thinking Press." University of Louisville. 2017. http://louisville.edu/ideastoaction/about/criticalthinking/framework

[xvii] The Foundation For Critical Thinking. *Valuable Intellectual Traits.* The Foundation for Critical Thinking. 2017. http://www.criticalthinking.org/pages/valuable-

intellectual-traits/528

xviii Ambler, George. *Learn to Think Long-Term Like Jeff Bezos*. George Ambler. 2014. http://www.georgeambler.com/learn-think-long-term-like-jeff-bezos/

xix Brown University. *Questions Provoking Critical Thinking*. Based on: "Alison King, "Inquiring Minds Really Do Want to Know: Using Questioning to Teach Critical Thinking," Teaching of Psychology 22 (1995): 14." Brown University. 2017. https://www.brown.edu/about/administration/sheridan-center/teaching-learning/effective-classroom-practices/discussions-seminars/questions

xx Serva, Christine. *Common Barriers to Critical Thinking*. Study. 2017. http://study.com/academy/lesson/common-barriers-to-critical-thinking.html

xxi Russel, Robert. *What Are Four Barriers to Critical Thinking?* Classroom. 2017. http://classroom.synonym.com/four-barriers-critical-thinking-8427849.html

xxii Austin, Michael W. Ph.D. *Standards of Critical Thinking*. Psychology Today. 2012. https://www.psychologytoday.com/blog/ethics-everyone/201206/standards-critical-thinking

xxiii Texas State University. Inconsistency. Texas State University. 2019. https://www.txstate.edu/philosophy/resources/f

allacy-definitions/Inconsistency.html

[xxiv] MacDonald, Chris. How can prejudice be a barrier that hinders critical thinking? Quora. 2018. https://www.quora.com/How-can-prejudice-be-a-barrier-that-hinders-critical-thinking

[xxv] Bain, Bruce R. How does peer influence constitute barriers to critical and creative thinking? Quora. 2016. https://www.quora.com/How-does-peer-influence-constitute-barriers-to-critical-and-creative-thinking

[xxvi] O'Reilley, Kim. Ph.D. *Why Critical Thinking Is So Important*. Intercultural Solutions. 2008. https://www.interculturalsolutions.net/why-critical-thinking-is-so-important/

[xxvii] Baer, Drake. *Here's How To Do Warren Buffett's Favorite Critical Thinking Exercise*. Business Insider. 2014. http://www.businessinsider.com/warren-buffetts-favorite-critical-thinking-exercise-2014-10

Made in the USA
San Bernardino, CA
24 November 2019